The Black Book of Speaking Fluent English

THE QUICKEST WAY TO IMPROVE YOUR SPOKEN ENGLISH

CHRISTOPHER HILL

Copyright © 2020 by Christopher Hill

All Rights Reserved

Disclaimer:

No part of this publication may be reproduced or transmitted in any form or by any means or transmitted electronically without direct written permission in writing from the author.

While all attempts have been made to verify the information provided in this publication, neither the author nor the publisher assumes any responsibility for errors, omissions, or misuse of the subject matter contained in this eBook.

This eBook is for entertainment purposes only, and the views expressed are those of the author alone, and should not be taken as expert instruction. The reader is responsible for their own actions.

Adherence to applicable laws and regulations, including international, federal, state, and local governing professional licensing business practices, advertising, and all other aspects of doing business in the U.S.A, Canada or any other jurisdiction is the sole responsibility of the purchaser or reader.

ACKNOWLEDGEMENTS

I want to express thanks to my committee for their continued support and encouragement: Dr. Hanson.G, my editors; Mary Smith; Carter Hoffman; and (illustrator) Mark Sherman. I offer my sincere appreciation for all the help provided by my committee.

My completion of this book could not have been accomplished without the support of my team, Albert, Johnny, and Amy. To Peter, and Rebeca. – thank you for allowing me time away from you to research and write. You guys deserve a trip to the Disneyland! Thanks to my parents as well, Mr. and Mrs. Hill. The countless times you kept the children during our hectic schedules will not be forgotten.

Finally, to my caring, loving, and supportive wife, Amy: my deepest gratitude. Your encouragement when the times got rough are much appreciated and noted. It was a great comfort and relief to know that you were willing to provide management of our household activities while I completed my work. My heartfelt thanks.

Contents

Acknowledgements iii

About the Author vii

Introduction x
What is Fluency? xii
Is English a Difficult Language to Learn? xii

Chapter 1: How Long Does Fluency Take? 1
Speaking English at Native Level
Will Take Time 2
The Art of Brain Rewiring 4
Immersing Yourself in English Completely 5

**Chapter 2: The 3 Golden Rules of Speaking
 Fluent English**....................................... 8
Think in English and Learn like a Baby 9
The Power of Immersion 11

Don't Be Afraid of Making Mistakes 12

Chapter 3: The Shadowing Technique Explained 14
What is The Shadowing Technique? 15
The Process of Shadowing....................................17
How Shadowing Will Greatly Improve
Your Spoken English 19

Chapter 4: Intensive Listening And How it Can Improve Your Fluency 21
What is Intensive Listening? 22
The Intensive Listening Method Explained 24
How Intensive Listening Will Improve
Your Spoken English 26

Chapter 5: The Importance of Learning Idioms And Slang 28
Why Idioms And Slang And Important
if You Want to be Fluent in English 29
What is an Idiom? 30
What is Slang? 32
Do Idioms and Slang Vary From
Region to Region? 34
How to Learn Common Idioms and
Slang Phrases 35

Chapter 6: How Grammar And Vocabulary Increase Fluency 43
Why Grammar Matters 45
How to Learn Grammar Without
Memorizing The Rules 47

How to Build a Lasting Vocabulary 50
The Power of Learning Phrases............................54
How to Memorize Your Vocabulary 56

Chapter 7: Accent Reduction Techniques............ 59
Shadowing - The Number One Way to
Reduce Your Accent 61
Listen to Your Own Voice And be
Mindful of Sounds 63

Chapter 8: The Key to Mastery 64
Understanding The Art of Repetition 65
The Three Steps to Mastering
English Fluency 66
Why You Shouldn't Expect Miracles
Overnight 68

**Bonus: Chapter 9: The Secret Method
to Become Super Fluent
in 21 Days 70**
Three Things You Need to Master First.............71
The Guidelines of The Fast Track Method........72
The Fast Track Method Explained -
21 Days to Fluency 73

Conclusion... 78

About the Author

Hello there! My name is Christopher Hill.

I have been an international English professor for more than 25 years, during which time I have taught at all levels, and many age groups from High School up to young adults. I have taught at a few big organizations in Japan, Vietnam, Germany and Taiwan, Universities, and technical colleges.

I have extensive experience teaching Business English in addition to General English. I also help ESL students prepare for English exams such as TOEFL iBT, IELTS, TOEIC and BEC.

I was an official examiner for IELTS, Cambridge Assessment and TEA. This allows me to assess my student's level and give my students a more custom and tailor-made approach for learning how to speak English more fluently.

I love helping others reach their language goals. I want students to feel confident, to have fun and to find relevancy in what we are doing!

I am extremely blessed to able to teach and support all of you in reaching your individual goals. As English has become such a crucial skill for connecting with the world at large - be it for business, education or pleasure –

Introduction

The ability to speak fluent English will revolutionize your life in ways you simply cannot see yet. Not only will you be able to travel to English-speaking countries and immerse yourself in the culture and way of life far easier, but you will open countless doors in terms of business and your career.

I am going to be the one to help you achieve fluency.

Let me introduce myself.

I am Christopher Hill and I am a highly experienced English professor of more than 25 years. Throughout my career, I have specialized in English speaking, helping many people, just like you, go from zero fluency to being able to hold a fluent conversation with an English native, without nerves or mistakes.

I have taught at several large educational institutions across Japan and China predominantly, as well as Open Universities, technical colleges, and even high schools. Throughout that time, I have taught a huge range of different students, all of whom managed to learn English as a second language.

They did it, and so can you.

I don't know your background, I can only assume that you are from a country which isn't English speaking, but you have a desire to learn fluent English in order to help you in your career, or because you simply want to take advantages of the many perks of being able to speak this most international of languages as fluently as possible. I should also point out that **this book isn't for beginners**, it is for those who already know a sufficient standard of English, but wish to speak more fluently.

Whatever your motivation, the key thing to remember is that if you put in the work, if you dedicate yourself to practice and understanding English at its very core, you will be able to achieve the holy grail - Fluency.

What is Fluency?

Fluency in any language is the ability to be able to hold a conversation with confidence, to use the correct words and combinations accurately, and to do it all with easy confidence. You are fluent in your native language, and you don't consciously think of which words to use and how to group them together because of its second nature to you. That is the core definition of fluency.

Whist learning a second language will probably never mean you're quite as confident or fluent as you are in your native language, you can aim for as close as possible. In ESL (English as a Second Language) terms, that's what we're going to be working towards in this book.

Is English a Difficult Language to Learn?

Many people who start to learn English either give up or fail to become fluent. In this case, they can speak English and get by, but they find it difficult to hold conversations and often make mistakes or misunderstand words spoken to them. This makes learning English even more difficult and leads to frustration and upset.

Most people can't achieve fluency because they aren't immersed in English, and because learning how to converse in English naturally actually involves a serious amount of practice. The rules that make up the very foundation of the English language bend and change according to the situation you're in and the conversation you're having and fluency requires you to understand this and use your logic to choose the right words and sentences.

Fluency does not happen overnight, but it can happen. The fact that most people don't achieve fluency isn't actually down to the difficulty level, it is completely down to motivation and practice. A little later in this book, I'm going to talk to you about how you can achieve English fluency in just three weeks - yes, three weeks. I will teach you an in-depth and intensive method which you can use at home by yourself, and with plenty of practice and dedication, you will be fluent in the English language by the end of those three weeks - just 21 short days.

I urge you to take your time reading this book and to make sure you understand every point made before moving on to the next section. If you need to make notes or re-read a section, there is no failing in that. Learning a language is difficult, but learning a language as prevalent as English, and to the level that we are aiming towards, requires motivation, dedication, and a commitment to many hours of practice. If you're happy to do all of that, I will take you from mediocre to fluent in just three weeks.

CHAPTER 1:

How Long Does Fluency Take?

Your journey towards English fluency starts now, but you might be wondering how long it will realistically take you to be able to speak this language completely confidently, without mistakes or worries.

Whilst I am going to show you a method which teaches you fluency in just three weeks, you can choose to work as slow or as fast as you like. It all comes down to how you learn, and the amount of time you can dedicate to your aim, alongside the regular day to day responsibilities that you have.

For some people, a slow approach works better, but for others, they want to absorb and practice as much as possible. This means they will achieve fluency far faster than those who prefer to work slowly.

Throughout my career, I have worked with a variety of different students, all of whom had different learning styles. Learning to understand your ideal learning speed will give you a general idea of how long it will take you to become fluent in English.

The best advice I can give is not to rush yourself, and to allow the natural learning process to take hold. If you are someone who learns slower and prefers to absorb as much information as possible, go with that. If you want to achieve faster results, put in the time and practice and you will achieve what you desire.

What you need to do is banish the idea that fluency is impossible from your mind. It might seem like staring the impossible in the face right now, effectively looking at climbing a mountain with little experience, but as you begin the learning process you are taking baby steps towards your final destination. Fluency is difficult and many people don't achieve it, but that isn't because it's impossible. Their failure to become fluent is down to a lack of time and effort.

Speaking English at Native Level Will Take Time

There is a difference between fluency and speaking English at the same level as a native. To succeed in your fluency aim, you need to understand this fact and discard unrealistic expectations.

The ability to speak English fluency means you speak confidently and accurately, but you will still need to think carefully before you verbalize words, no matter what situation you are in. On the other hand, the native level means speaking English in the same easy-going way that you speak your first language.

For instance, if you speak Japanese as your native language, you don't have to stop and think about the words you need to use to answer a person's question. You don't have to quickly go through grammar rules in your mind and you don't have any hesitation between being asked a question and answering it. This is because you are a native speaker, and that is the difference between fluency and native level. Fluency means there will always be a slight hesitation, but it isn't enough to interfere with the flow of understanding of the conversation on either side.

It is entirely possible to learn to speak English at a native level, but this is going to take a lot of time and effort. The method I am going to demonstrate to you a little later in this book will take you three weeks to master, but that is certainly not going to take you to the native level. To reach a natural native level, you will need to reach fluency first, and then continue to practice with native English speakers. You will also need to immerse yourself in an English environment if you wish to achieve a native language level.

The Art of Brain Rewiring

Learning a new language requires a new wiring route in your brain. You currently have one language within your brain, and as you have been speaking that language since you were a child, that is the go-to language your brain chooses when it wants to verbalize a need, feeling, or simply to converse with another person.

When you choose to learn another language, many studies have shown that you need to rewire part of your brain, to store all the information about that language, such as vocabulary, grammar, etc. When you switch between two languages, as you will be doing if you are fluent in English and your first language, this triggers a completely different type of brain activity, compared to if you were simply using one language to converse. The main area of your brain associated with language and speech is the prefrontal cortex, and this is where the rewiring needs to be done.

The good news is that many studies have also found that learning another language, even as an adult, can help your brain remain strong and stave off the possible effects of age-related cognitive decline, such as Alzheimer and dementia. The process of learning a new language forms new connections and pathways to form within the brain, and the more you practice and learn, the stronger these connections become.

Whilst it is certainly easier to learn another language earlier in life, it is still entirely possible to do so as you get older, and it is never too late to develop and rewire your brain as a result. You don't need to do any specific cognitive exercises to achieve this rewiring effect, you simply need to practice and dedicate time to learning English as a second language. Of course, if you can immerse yourself in English as much as possible, you'll help to speed up the process and formulate those connections in your brain much faster too.

Immersing Yourself in English Completely

I just touched upon the idea of immersing yourself in English as much as you possibly can. I appreciate that not everyone can do this, but you have the added benefit of the Internet. In that case, you have a huge advantage over anyone who was attempting to learn English two decades ago.

If you can practice your English-speaking skills with a native English speaker, you will find the process of achieving fluency occurs must faster. This is because you will subconsciously take cues from the other person and build up your confidence levels at the same time. Never underestimate the power of confidence when it comes to learning any language, not only English.

If you don't have the opportunity to speak to a native English speaker, make sure that you watch English speaking movies, using the subtitles option to help you build connections between the words in your native language, whilst listening to the English words and how they are pronounced. What you do need to be aware of in this situation is accents.

Native English speakers do not have one accent alone. The main native English-speaking countries of the United Kingdom, the USA, Canada, Australia, and New Zealand all contain various regions, and within those regions, you will find quite distinct accents. For example, in England alone, you will hear a huge difference between the accent of someone from the city of Liverpool or Newcastle, compared to someone who was born and raised in London or Birmingham. The same can be said for the various states across the USA.

Many people in the UK do not speak the Queen's English, i.e. the cut-glass English accent you will hear spoken on TV shows depicting Victorian times. Despite that, the grammar rules remain the same. Avoiding slang phrases is a vital part of the puzzle.

You can also opt to read children's books in English. This is one of the classic methods of learning any language because it helps you to form connections in your brain between the written word and the way the letters are formed in speech. If you do this, you will find that your fluency of English is far higher quality than someone who focuses on speech alone, rather than the written words as a package.

By immersing yourself in the world of a native English speaker, you will speed up the learning process, provided you also put forth the time and effort required.

CHAPTER 2:

The 3 Golden Rules of Speaking Fluent English

To learn to speak English fluently, you need to practice consistently, but you also need to avoid pitfalls and know how to speed up the process. There are three specific rules which I always teach my students, all of which speed up the fluency process, but also ensure a higher degree of accuracy.

You can rush the process of learning to speak fluently as much as you like, but if you're speaking English incorrectly, it will have been a total waste of your time and effort. It is far better to ensure accuracy and care, to give you a firm foundation on which to build.

There are three golden rules you must follow when attempting to learn English fluently:

- Think in the English language, learning as if you were a baby
- Immerse yourself in the English language and its culture
- Never be afraid to make mistakes

Let's explore each rule in turn.

Think in English and Learn like a Baby

One of the greatest challenges for an adult learner is the ability to relinquish control and realize that to achieve their aim, they need to go back to learning as a child. This can be difficult for many adults to do, because it somehow makes them feel inferior, or lacking in knowledge.

The bottom line is that you do not know English fluently at this point, but if you take the time to learn, you will. Learning requires starting at zero, i.e. starting at the point of no knowledge. This is how a child is born and grows. From zero they move up the incremental ladder and finally arrive at expert knowledge of the subject they're attempting to master. They may never be an expert, but they came along way to reach their destination.

This is how you need to approach learning fluent English. Repetition and practice are the building blocks of learning, and these are elements you have been implementing since you were a child, learning whatever was placed in front of you.

It's also important to attempt to think in English as much as possible. If you can try and change your mindset from thinking your native language to thinking in English, or at least attempting to think in both, you are forcing your brain to create those new connections, speeding up the rewiring process.

A good piece of advice I always give to my students is to read the road and street signs in English, and if they are not written in English, to translate the language to English in your mind. Try your best to avoid conversations in your head in your native language; this is something you can do with your eyes closed, but attempting it in English will take more time and effort - this is a practice you are doing without even realizing it and it will create stronger connections in less time.

The Power of Immersion

In our last chapter, I mentioned that immersing yourself in English and the English culture is something that will solidify your language efforts. This is something you should not overlook or underestimate. Doing this will also help you to think in English far easier because the culture and language are everywhere you turn.

Again, I appreciate that not everyone will be in a position to immerse themselves completely, but allowing yourself to do this as much as possible will certainly aid your efforts and speed up your fluency. There is bound to be someone within your city who speaks English, even if not fluently. Approach them and ask if you can practice your conversational skills with them.

There is a reason that language courses based in the country of the language being spoken are so popular. For instance, learning to speak Spanish in Spain will be far easier than attempting to learn Spanish in China. The reason is that you are compete surrounded by the language, both verbally and in the written word. It seeps its way into your subconscious and you will begin thinking in the language without even realizing it.

If you are in a position to travel and do this, I would urge you to do so. If you aren't in this position, immersing yourself as much as possible will certainly aid your efforts.

Don't Be Afraid of Making Mistakes

The final golden rule I always stress to all of my students is never to be afraid of mistakes.

Mistakes allow you to learn. When you make a mistake, you learn how not to do something. This experience will allow you to understand how that mistake felt, and you will be far less likely to repeat it in the future, as a result of being immersed in that experience.

The fear of making mistakes often stops students from practicing, but this is not going to help your efforts. You are going to make mistakes when you attempt to speak English fluently. You cannot avoid it. When you were a child and you were starting to learn how to talk, you no doubt made countless mistakes, and your teacher or your parents would gently tell you the right way to say a word. From there, you might have made the mistake a couple of times more, but in the end, you understood and rectified the problem. This is the same way you need to learn and focus on the issue at hand.

Without mistakes, you cannot learn the right way to do something, and there is no English student on this planet who has never made a mistake before!

Embrace your mistakes and see them as progress towards your goal of fluency in English. It shows a willingness to try, a willingness to take risks, and those risks will be rewarded over time.

CHAPTER 3:

The Shadowing Technique Explained

The first practical tip I'm going to discuss is regarding shadowing.

Shadowing is a technique which allows you to understand how you are pronouncing particular words and sounds, and ensuring that you are correctly doing this. A word can be completely changed in meaning and tone by pronouncing it incorrectly.

You will already know that the English language isn't necessarily phonetic, i.e. you cannot always rely upon pronouncing a word exactly how it sounds. There are many combinations of letters that care different sounds to how they appear on their own; for instance, the word "gnome". This word has a silent "g", and pronouncing this phonetically would be incorrect. In this case, you would pronounce the word "nome".

Without hearing a word such as "gnome" being spoken by a native speaker of English, you would probably have no idea about the silent first letter. English is full of small anomalies such as this, and shadowing is an advanced technique that allows you to ensure that you are covering all bases in terms of these slight breaks in the rules, and you're also pronouncing letters and overall words correctly.

Shadowing can be done with the help of a native speaker in person, or it can be done via a tape or audio recording. Most learners choose to go down the route of an audio recording because this allows you to take your time to listen to the sounds and the pronunciation without distraction. However, if you prefer to work one on one with a native speaker, someone who can correct you gently if you make a slight mistake, this is also a good option to try.

What is The Shadowing Technique?

The shadowing technique involves you listening to a sentence in English and speaking it aloud whilst you're listening to it. This allows you to effectively copy the speaker/tape, and listen to the sounds they're making, compared to how you're verbalizing them. The word "shadowing" comes from the fact that you are effectively following their lead.

As you can see, shadowing sounds very easy in theory, but in practice, it can be a little more difficult and requires a lot of concentration and practice. You need to be completely focused on the speech you're hearing and work to replicate it back quickly and accurately. Of course, if you opt for a tape or other audio recording, you can easily rewind the section and practice it over as many times as you need, until you get the words correctly pronounced.

Shadowing is also a very effective way to reduce your accent. Regardless of which country you are originally from, you will have an accent of some kind, and when speaking English this can change the sound of certain letters and words in many cases. By shadowing, you're learning how to verbalize the sounds as a native would, therefore effectively adopting an English accent when repeating the words back. This is ideal for reducing a heavily affected accent.

When choosing the type of recording or person to practice with, you should, however, ensure that they have an easy to understand accent themselves. If you choose someone with a heavy regional accent, you are going to end up repeating back the words with the same inflections they use. As a result, you're going to shadow their accent and develop it as they have. For instance, if you are listening to a person from Birmingham speaking and you're shadowing their words, you are going to slowly start to develop a Birmingham accent if you continue to use this person's speech to develop your fluency.

If you want to learn how to speak English effectively, it's best to choose a recording or person who has no heavy accent, e.g. avoid strong regional accents. The good news is that most English speakers, accent or no accent, can speak very clearly if you ask them to.

The Process of Shadowing

I've explained what shadowing is, but you also need to know the step by step guide on how to actually do it.

Assuming you are going to use an audio recording to try the shadowing technique, all you need is the recording and a way to play it, e.g. iPod and downloaded recordings, a pair of headphones to cancel out background noise, and a quiet space where you can speak freely.

It is best to opt for a recording that contains a page of native English speech, and if you can choose a topic that interests you, you'll find it easier and more interesting to shadow the words being spoken.

Listen to the text to completion once, without speaking. This will allow you to know what the piece is about, without surprises, and allow you to shadow the words far easier. If you need to listen once or twice more, that's fine; make sure you're comfortable with the content before you begin speaking

If you hear any words you're not sure of, or words you don't understand, note them down and then look them up before you begin speaking. This will help develop your confidence and allow you to use that word more freely in future

Now, listen to the text and repeat it as quickly as you can after the words are spoken. This doesn't mean rushing, as the whole point is to ensure you're pronouncing the words correctly, but simply try your best to keep up with the tempo

Repeat the recording a few more times, until you're comfortable with all the words you've learned and their correct pronunciation. It's entirely normal to repeat the text multiple times

Many people use the shadowing technique on the same piece of text until they have almost committed it to memory and this is something which is advisable to do. By repeating words to the point where they are ingrained in your memory, you will find it easier to be able to pronounce all letters and words together in the future. This will also increase your confidence to a large degree, putting you on the road towards fluency.

How Shadowing Will Greatly Improve Your Spoken English

Shadowing is a technique that I highly recommend to all of my students and one which will give you great confidence in speaking English fluently. By practicing a section of text until you can recall it by memory, you are effectively committing the sounds and pronunciation to memory also. The next time you hear the same sound, you will understand instantly, and you will repeat it correctly, ironing out any potential pronunciation issues immediately.

As I have already mentioned, shadowing is also ideal for flattening out an accent and allowing you to speak English fluently, as an English person would. English affected by a heavy accent from another country can change the sounds and meaning in some cases, but when you shadow the words and sounds from a native English speaker, you're learning the way the sounds should be pronounced as close to perfect as possible.

Shadowing does take time and practice, but it is a process which is more than worth it, and one which will drastically decrease the amount of time it takes you to go from your current English speaking level, to fluency level.

Whilst shadowing does focus on the meaning of the text to a certain degree, this is more to help you understand and engage with the text, more than actually needing to understand what it means. Shadowing is about pronunciation and allowing you to speak correctly, without any errors you may have picked up earlier in your learning process, and allowing them to continue as you gain the confidence to speak English freely.

In the next chapter, we will discuss another intensive exercise that works side by side with shadowing, allowing you to understand pronunciation and increase your vocabulary. This is called intensive listening.

CHAPTER 4:

Intensive Listening And How it Can Improve Your Fluency

Another very useful technique when attempting to become fluent in any language, not just English, is intensive listening. When used alongside shadowing, intensive listening can greatly increase your fluency skills, by helping you to pronounce sounds and words correctly, whilst also building up your vocabulary of words and how best to use them.

There are two main types of listening which any student wishing to become fluent should do - intensive listening and extensive listening. In this chapter, I'm going to focus on intensive listening, as this is known to help ensure confidence and build up fluency far faster as a result.

Many people overlook the importance of listening. You might think that to become fluent in English you need to focus on speaking and practicing, and whilst that's certainly true to a large degree, listening will allow you to learn far more than you realize. For instance, in the last chapter, I highlighted the fact that in the English language, there are many silent letters, and pronouncing them will make the word completely wrong. This could even change the meaning in some situations. Intensive listening will help you to understand the nuances of the English language, and therefore improve your fluency skills far faster.

What is Intensive Listening?

Do you know how to listen? Most people think they understand how to listen and exercise the methods very well, but in reality, they simply hear the words. When words float into one ear, linger in the brain for a few seconds without being acknowledged, and then float back out the other ear, you're not really hearing or understanding the words. You're simply hearing the sounds. As a result, you're not paying half as much attention as you should be.

Learning how to listen properly will ensure that you become fluent in English far faster than if you stick with allowing words to float in and out of your ears. This allows you to understand the meaning, build your vocabulary, and allow you to feel far more confident and free when speaking.

Intensive listening, as the name suggests, focuses on an intense, short burst of English. On the other hand, extensive listening allows you to listen and understand a longer speech. Intensive listening is very beneficial because the short length forces you to concentrate and complete focus on the words you're hearing.

Intensive listening usually lasts for a few minutes at most, but you need to focus completely. This means using this type of exercise somewhere quiet and where you're not going to be disturbed, in order to allow you to concentrate completely.

When you're using intensive listening, you need to focus on:

- Pronunciation of sounds and words
- Grammar and how the rules shift and change according to context
- Vocabulary, i.e. the words used and different words which can be used to mean the same thing

This type of exercise isn't really about understanding the meaning of the text, it's about focusing on the three factors above. Intensive listening, therefore, helps you to build up the groundwork, and when used with shadowing also, you're building on your skills step by step.

The Intensive Listening Method Explained

I've just talked about what you need to listen to when using the intensive listening technique, but now I need to highlight exactly how to do it.

Sit somewhere quiet, and make sure that you're not going to be disturbed. The art of listening means that you need to focus all of your attention on the thing you're hearing, and if you have half an ear on background noise, or waiting for your telephone to ring, and half an ear on the text you're listening to, you're not going to pick up on all the subtle points you need to hear.

You will need a pair of headphones and again, just like with shadowing, a tape or recording which is suitable for intensive listening exercises. You can download many of these online, or you can find CDs from libraries or bookshops.

There are many websites these days that allow you to link images with the words you're hearing, but as you already have a good standard of English and you are focusing your efforts on becoming fluent, these may be a little below your standard at this current time. Simplify things down and instead stick to a recording.

As with the shadowing exercise I discussed in the last chapter, be very wary of accents. Sounds change hugely between accents, and to hear the crystal clear pronunciation of a word, you need a clear accent. Most recordings will tell you the accent of the person you will be listening to, so this is something to be on the lookout for.

All you need to do then is sit quietly and listen to the short passage. You need to really focus and tune in to every single word, examining the sounds and pronunciation of the word. Don't stop the recording halfway through, make sure you listen from start to finish, but you should then go back over it and repeat the process, to solidify what you have learned in your mind.

If there are any words you aren't sure of, once you've listened to a couple of times and you're sure you haven't grasped their proper pronunciation, you can look these words up and practice them individually.

The beauty of intensive listening is in its flexibility and the fact that it allows you to focus on the nuances of the English language, such as grammatical changes, therefore increasing your fluency skills.

How Intensive Listening Will Improve Your Spoken English

The ability to understand the differences in language and how they change according to what is being said, and how the sentence is being constructed, allows you to understand English at its very core.

Conversational English can sometimes be quite different from the English you will learn when you start your language journey. Intensive listening allows you to tune into those differences, and this is partly what will allow you to become a better English speaker as a result.

Whilst intensive listening isn't really about the meaning of the passage you're listening to, because it's designed to be short and intensive in concentration, it does help if you are listening to something which you enjoy. For instance, choose a subject which calls out to your interest levels and you're more likely to listen closely. This can become more difficult if the subject matter is technical or something you don't particularly enjoy.

Intensive listening can improve your fluency by allowing you to understand English 'as is'. By using shadowing techniques at the same time, you'll find that your fluency level increases much faster as a result. If you want to add in advanced listening, which focuses on longer portions of speech, you can do that once you've mastered the art of intensive listening first.

Put simply, learning how to really listen will teach you to speak English in a far more authentic and accurate way.

CHAPTER 5:

The Importance of Learning Idioms And Slang

Every single language on the planet has differences across regions, but all languages also have slang phrases and idioms which are important to learn if you want to really understand what is being said to you in conversation.

By learning idioms and slang, you're more able to speak English like a native would, i.e. you can take part in-jokes, you will understand what someone says without taking offense, and it basically increases your level of fluency to a higher degree.

The English language has a huge number of common idioms and slang phrases and many of them vary from country to country and region to region. For instance, the idioms you will hear in the UK may be completely different from the idioms you'll hear in other native English speaking countries, such as Australia or the USA. It really depends on where you will be living, who you will be speaking to, where you will be traveling, or the countries you're going to be doing business with, in terms of which idioms and slang phrases you need to master first and foremost.

Why Idioms And Slang And Important if You Want to be Fluent in English

It is important to realize that you will never learn all the idioms and slang phrases within one country, let along all across the native English speaking world. There are always new phrases entering into the language, but it's a good idea to know the most common, i.e. the ones which everyone tends to fall back on.

The reason is that it allows you to speak far more naturally and to converse with native English speakers on their native level. In a moment I'm going to cover exactly what an idiom and slang phrase is, and why they're so important in the modern world, but for now, you need to understand that if you want to speak English fluently, following the grammatical rules to the letter and learning the so-called "Queen's English" will not allow you to be fluent.

A fluent English speaker speaks in a way that a native might. Of course, a fluent speaker isn't going to have the same proficiency as a native speaker, because to them the language is second nature, but they will be able to hold a conversation in much the same way. Once you start using shadowing and intensive listening exercises, as I have covered in the last two chapters, you'll start to see just how important idioms and slang phrases are in the English language.

A conversation usually includes several of both, and if you want to understand the meaning of the conversation, you need to know the idioms and slang. Most of the time, idioms and slang phrases have no close meaning to the words being spoken. For instance, "get off my back" is an idiom, but it means "leave me alone"; it has nothing to do with touching someone's back!

What is an Idiom?

I've just given you a prime example of an idiom, with "get off my back". An idiom is a phrase that doesn't hold the same meaning as the words being said.

For instance, "you hit the nail on the head" is a common idiom. This has nothing to do with hammering nails into a wall, it means "you're right". The English language is full of idioms and learning the most common will help you grasp an understanding of a conversation, without completely misunderstanding the person you're conversing with.

Another common idiom is "we're all in the same boat". You will hear this a lot when listening to native English speakers conversing with each other and speaking about a particular problem. This could also be heard when listening to work-related conversations. This idiom has nothing to do with boats, and instead, it means something akin to "we all have the same problem", or "we're all in the same situation".

A little later I'm going to give you some of the most common idioms you can begin to learn, but again, it's important to realize that you're never going to master them all. There are countless, and if you do hear something which you suspect to be an idiom, but you're not sure of the meaning, it's a good idea to ask the person you're speaking to what it actually means. By doing this, you'll expand your vocabulary and you'll increase your fluency skills. Never be afraid to ask questions, this is how you will learn more.

One of the biggest pointers that you're actually listening to an idiom you've never heard before is if it doesn't fit into the sentence or conversation you're listening to at all. For instance, "we're all in the same boat" could be used when talking about a big problem at work, and if you've understood the conversation up to that point, and then someone throws this idiom into the chat, you will understand you're dealing with an idiom because boats make no sense in context!

Understanding idioms is a vital part of English fluency because they allow you to understand the conversation completely.

What is Slang?

Alongside idioms, you will also hear a lot of slang phrases whilst listening to conversational English. Slang is used across the world in all different countries, but the phases used are totally different in each. In our next section, I'm going to explain that theory a little more, but for now, we need to focus on what slang is and why you need to learn it.

Slang is an informal way of saying something. For instance, you will hear many English people saying "innit" when they mean "isn't it". You will also hear this completely out of context, possibly at the end of a sentence, asking for the other person's agreement.

Slang is often used as a way to form an identity, e.g. members of a certain group will use slang phrases within their social setting. This is mostly seen in schools, with certain age groups using specific types of slang to hold them together.

You could argue that slang is a lazy way to speak, but it's been around for so long that it is ingrained in every single language out there. You will also see several slang phrases making it into the dictionary these days because they're so common and part of everyday life. For instance, the word "rank" is often used in English to say something is disgusting. Now, rank is a word in its own right and has nothing to do with whether something is unpleasant, so this type of slang is also an idiom.

As a result, learning idioms and slang is vital if you want to master English fluency and understand what is being said to you. The more you can use common types of idioms and slang, the more you'll be able to converse fluently with native English speakers too.

Slang is something you will tend to hear more in speech than you will see in writing. Apart from texts, you won't often see slang appearing in written English, but you may find idioms in a casual form of writing.

Do Idioms and Slang Vary From Region to Region?

A little earlier I touched upon the fact that certain slang phrases may be used by people in a certain group or region, and that's a common fact. Idioms can be regional, but these tend to be more widely known. Slang, however, is something you will find varying from region to region.

You will find different slang phrases in the USA to what you will find in Australia, you will find different slang phrases in New Zealand to what you will find in the UK. The more you spend time immersed in each particular country, the more you will pick up on these useful phrases and be able to use them in your own speech, therefore increasing your own fluency level.

Unless you plan to base yourself in one specific city, it's probably not going to be of any use to you to learn very regional idioms or slang phrases. I would recommend learning the most common and widespread options, to help you move from place to place, and increase your fluency as you go. This will help you to widen your net in terms of who you can converse with and doesn't give you unnecessary limitations.

How to Learn Common Idioms and Slang Phrases

The next question is how to actually learn idioms and slang phrases. These aren't things you will find in textbooks and recordings, and they are things you will need to pick up by immersing yourself in English as much as you can.

Watching English films will allow you to learn many idioms, so it may be a good idea to use subtitles to allow you to pick up on context and understand when a phrase doesn't fit in with meaning. In this case, you're likely dealing with an idiom. A good rule of thumb is to use subtitles in English whilst listening to the words. Whilst it might take your attention away from what is happening in the film, you will be able to match written words up to the sounds, therefore giving you a shadowing exercise without actually realizing it.

Listening to English speakers will also allow you to pick up idioms and slang phrases, and if you don't understand something, simply ask and most people will be happy to explain what the phrase means. This is a great way of learning.

For those who find it difficult to immerse themselves completely in the English language, e.g. they do not have any native English speakers around them, it really comes down to watching TV programs. Thankfully, the Internet has allowed us to watch any program, no matter where we are in the world, and this is a blessing in terms of learning to recognize and understand specific idioms and slang phrases, in your journey towards English fluency.

To help you get started with learning the most common idioms and slang phrases, below you will find a list to focus on. Remember, this is by no means an exhaustive list, and new idioms and slang phrases appear all the time. These will allow you to understand how idioms work and will give you a starting vocabulary of slang phrases in the English language generally.

Common Idioms to Learn

Whilst idioms will vary across native English speaking countries, the ones below are common in the English speaking world in general. You will hear them just as frequently in the US as you will in the UK, Australia, etc.

- A blessing in disguise - Something which seems bad at first, but turns out to be a good thing
- Better late than never - It is better to arrive a little late than never to arrive
- Bite the bullet - Do something you don't want to do, but have to do
- Break a leg - Good luck
- Cut me some slack - Don't be so hard on me
- Easy does it - Take it easy, slow down
- Getting out of hand - Something is getting a little out of control
- Back to the drawing board - Go back to the beginning of something
- Hang on in there - Don't give up
- Hit the sack - Go to bed
- To make a long story short - To say something quickly
- You've missed the boat - You're too late
- On the ball - You're doing a good job

- You can't have the best of both worlds - You can't have everything

- Feeling under the weather - Feeling a little ill

- You can say that again - I agree

- We'll cross that bridge when we come to it - We'll solve that problem when we need to, not right now

- To add insult to injury - To make things worse

- You're barking up the wrong tree - You have the wrong idea

- A perfect storm - The worst possible situation

- You made it by the skin of your teeth - You got there just in time

- That cost an arm and a leg - That was very expensive

- Every cloud has a silver lining - Something good usually comes after something bad

- Don't put all your eggs in one basket - Don't focus on just one thing

- Cold shoulder - To ignore

- Bigger fish to fry - Something bigger to concentrate on
- Look before you leap - Think things through before you do something
- You're skating on thin ice - You're taking unnecessary risks
- Once in a blue moon - Something which happens rarely
- I'll take a rain check - To postpone something
- Get your act together - Do something better

From this list, you can see how idioms work. The meaning is completely different from the words being spoken. Learning to understand the most common idioms in the English language will allow you to understand the conversation, and therefore increase your fluency to a large degree.

Common Slang Phrases to Learn

Because slang is so widely used and differs from country to country and even region to region, for the purposes of this section, I'm going to concentrate on some of the most common UK phrases you will hear. These do tend to filter down to other English-speaking countries to a certain degree, so understanding them will give you a head start on your fluency level.

- Chuffed - Very happy
- Knackered - Tired
- Shattered - Tired
- Cuppa - A cup of tea
- Mate - Friend
- Innit - Isn't it? Looking for agreement
- Famished - Hungry
- Starving - Hungry
- Cheeky - Disrespectful but in a lighthearted way
- Gutted - Disappointed
- Fluke - Something which has happened by luck or chance
- Gagging - Thirsty
- Awesome - Really great
- Cool - Very good
- Hang out - Meet up socially

- Chill out - Relax
- Sick - Whilst this can mean ill, in slang, it's more likely to mean something is very good
- Epic - Huge
- Dunno - I don't know
- Rip off - To buy something expensive that wasn't worth the money
- Catch you later - Goodbye
- Make fun of - To tease or joke
- Gig - A show or a job
- Dough - Money
- A ball - Having a good time
- Nuts - Crazy
- Hot - Attractive
- Chicken - A coward
- Neat - Very good
- Couch potato - A lazy person
- An earful - A scolding

- Bummed - Disappointed or sad
- Flicks - The cinema

The more slang words you can understand and use, the more you will sound fluent when speaking English to a native speaker. Of course, that doesn't mean you should pepper your sentences with slang too much because that could make you sound unprofessional in the wrong setting. Simply stick to the odd phrase here and there, and follow the lead of the person you're speaking to, as to whether this is a slang-appropriate situation or not.

Conversations with employees, in formal settings, or with people of importance are not likely to include slang, and in these situations, you should avoid slang phrases altogether unless you know them personally.

CHAPTER 6:

How Grammar And Vocabulary Increase Fluency

Because you can already speak English a little, you will know that English grammar is not the easiest to learn and understand. Whilst certainly not the most difficult language in the world, the changing rules of English grammar can make it difficult to understand and use correctly.

The bottom line is that grammar is necessary if you want to speak English correctly and fluently. Without grammar, you're going to be using the wrong choice of words, in the wrong situation, and it is going to make your spoken English sound very basic, and in some cases, extremely difficult to understand.

The problem is, grammar seems like a mountain that cannot be climbed. That's not the case, you simply need to understand how to use grammar correctly, without being too pushed down by all the rules. That is something I am going to teach you in this chapter.

Firstly, what is grammar?

Grammar is the structure of a language, the rules which make it understandable to others. Grammar is also the study of words. It tells you how to use words in specific sentences, and how to use words to change meanings. Grammar also changes according to the situation, which is the main issue people learning to speak English fluently struggle with.

The fact that English isn't your native language puts you at somewhat of a disadvantage. When native English speakers learn their home language, they learn grammar when they are very young, and they learn it in a way that seems almost forgettable. If you ask most native English speakers about the rules of grammar, they may not be able to tell you. This is because they learned their language via immersion and early school years education. The fact you need to understand grammatical rules and changes as an adult can be more difficult, but it also means that you have the chance to learn grammar correctly, therefore increasing the quality of your fluency.

Why Grammar Matters

Without grammar, there are no rules. That means your speech would be a mess. There would be no pauses where a full stop would go, there would be no capital letters in written English, there would be incorrect endings placed on words, making them somewhat unrecognizable, and overall, people would struggle to understand your point.

Whilst we're focusing on spoken English, for a second let me demonstrate the power of grammar in the written English word.

Let's take the phrase "you are". You will already know that you can combine "you" and "are" by using an apostrophe, creating "you're". Being able to do this will help your fluency in speech, but also writing. No native speaker says "you are late" unless they're angry, they're far more likely to say "you're late". Understanding this will increase your fluency once more.

Now, when the apostrophe in "you're" is placed in the wrong place, and the entire meaning of the sentence changes in a big way.

For instance:

"look at your hair" versus "look at you're hair".

These are two different sentences with one being completely grammatically incorrect.

"Their" and "they're" are also commonly muddled up words in English. "Their" means something which belongs to them. "They're" means "they are".

This is why grammar matters so much - getting one small apostrophe in the wrong place can not only change the meaning in some cases but will create a poor sense of your English fluency in all cases. If you're trying to make a great impression and you get this point wrong, you're not going to achieve your aim.

The problem is, attempting to get all the grammar rules right can cause stress and second-guessing, which hampers your fluency efforts. By trying to get every single sentence grammatically correct, your speech is going to be stilted and slow, not at all fluent. You may also end up making your English overly correct, i.e. not really conversational. Most English speakers do not get every single grammatical rule correct when speaking in their daily lives; by attempting to do so, you're not going to sound fluent!

By all means, learn the rules if you want to, but focusing on how your English sounds and ensuring that your sentences are created correctly in terms of how someone would understand them, is a far better way forward.

Let's discuss this point a little more.

How to Learn Grammar Without Memorizing The Rules

Learning to speak fluent English requires a certain amount of knowledge of the grammatical rules to follow, but this doesn't require you to memorize them completely. Instead, I recommend learning by listening.

I mentioned the advanced and intensive listening methods a little earlier and these are both a fantastic way to learn grammar, without having to sit there and understand the many different rules which make up the English language. Shadowing will also allow you to do this.

The bottom line is that English grammar isn't easy. It's not the most difficult language in the world, but the rules often change according to context and what you want to say. There are set rules, but there are equally as many anomalies to those rules. Trying to learn them all is going to cause you to become extremely overwhelmed and will hamper your efforts to speak English fluently.

It's a good idea to understand tenses completely. If you get your tenses wrong, the entire sentence you're trying to speak changes its meaning completely. For instance:

- "I went to the supermarket" - This is a past tense sentence informing someone that you went to the supermarket, i.e. you have already been
- "I go to the supermarket" - This could mean you're about to go, or you sometimes go. The meaning is ambiguous and isn't something a fluent speaker would use
- "I will go to the supermarket" - This means you are going to go to the supermarket at some point in the near future

Can you see how different they are in meaning? It's very easy for someone to misunderstand what you are trying to say if you don't learn tenses. It's also vital that you learn about nouns and verbs, i.e. naming words and doing words, as well as adjectives, also known as descriptive words. But, should you go into all of the other quite complicated rules?

Not necessarily.

By all means, if you want to learn to speak English on a native level, you will need to understand grammar, but as I mentioned before, most native speakers wouldn't be able to explain grammar rules to you either. They have learned by practice and they have a second nature for understanding what sounds correct, and what doesn't. This is something I urge you to do, rather than trying to spend a huge amount of time understanding the specific grammar rules.

You will easily pick up the basics by shadowing, using specific listening exercises, and looking into any words and phrases that you come across during these exercises. Once you're listening or shadowing, listen to the meaning and be curious. If something doesn't make sense to you, or it's a word or phrase you've never heard before, look it up and research it. This is a far better way to ensure your fluency and correct grammar, than spending endless hours trying to understand rules which bend and change according to context.

How to Build a Lasting Vocabulary

Your vocabulary is the number of words you know, which you use to form a sentence and speak to other people. It, therefore, stands to reason that the more words you know, and the better you know how to use them, the more fluent you will become. Building a lasting vocabulary is about three things:

- Introducing yourself to new words
- Understanding what they mean
- Practicing them until they are memorized

When you come across a word you haven't heard before, look it up and learn more about it. Be inquisitive and try to understand meanings and sounds. You should then practice how to stay the word, by making sure that you're pronouncing it correctly. After that, once you've grasped the meaning and how to say the word correctly, use it in conversation to build your confidence.

A thesaurus is a great tool for learning new words. This is similar to a dictionary but it gives you alternative words, which have the same meaning. For instance, if you were looking up the word "hot", a thesaurus may show you the following words:

- Steaming
- Boiling
- Heat
- Blistering
- Broiling
- Burning
- Fiery
- Scorching

These words all mean the same thing in certain contexts, and they allow you to build your vocabulary. Why not look up several words per day as part of your routine, and find new words to add to your collection? This is an exercise that I have always found to bring great results.

The best ways to develop a large and lasting vocabulary therefore are:

- Use a thesaurus to find alternative words with the same meaning
- Commit to looking up five new words in your thesaurus per day

- Look up words you don't know the meaning of immediately and practice them until you feel confident

- Watch English films and TV shows to find out new words, and again, look them up to find out what they mean, practicing how to say them

- Read a little every day and find new words to look up and learn

- Keep a word journal. This means writing down the new words you learn every day and repeating them until they are committed to your memory

- Try doing word puzzles in English. Try word searches first as these are the easiest option. This will give you a list of words to find, and some of those words may be new to you. You could then move on to crossword or criss-cross puzzles, which will also give you new vocabulary additions to think about

- Play word games. You can easily find many word games online or even as apps on your phone. These will allow you to diversify your current vocabulary and learn many new words

- In conversation, if someone says a word you've never heard before, ask them what it means and then write it down to think about later

These are all ways you can add new words to your vocabulary, but how do you memorize them, to use them in the future?

As children, we learn by repetition. This means that the more you say or hear something, the more it will be committed to your memory. When you hear a new word, it's important that you note it down. The act of actually writing the word down, even if it's a phonetic spelling at that point, will etch it into your short-term memory. Then, when you have the time, look the word up, learn what it means, and find out how to say it correctly. After that, it's a case of repetition.

Say the word a few times, find sentences that fit the word, and use it as much as possible. I mentioned using a word journal, and looking at this every day will help you remember new words too.

At the end of the day, however, practice really does make perfect, and that means the more you use words, the more easily you will remember them in future conversations.

It is very easy to commit to learning the basics of English, but even if you can pronounce the basics very well, that is never going to make you fluent. A fluent speaker has a range of words and phrases (more on that shortly) in their vocabulary and can mix and match them according to the situation.

For instance, there are formal ways to say things and informal ways. You would use a formal type of vocabulary if you were speaking to your manager or someone in power. For instance, "the weather is very changeable today" is a formal way of saying "it rains, then it's sunny, I wish it would stop". The two sentences mean the same thing, but according to who you're speaking to and the situation you're in, it depends upon how you say it and the words you choose. A larger, committed to memory vocabulary will allow you to satisfy these types of situations with ease, and increase your fluency.

The Power of Learning Phrases

A little earlier I talked about the power of idioms, and how you should learn them if you want to understand the meaning of conversations and texts and use them as much as you can, in order to increase your own fluency. In this case, I want to talk about why it's important to learn phrases and not just words.

When learning any language, it's easy to stick to memorizing single words, because this is an easier option and helps you understand the general gist of a conversation. The problem with English is that words can change their meaning according to the context they're being used in. For that reason, it's important to learn and understand phrases just as much.

The idiom "it's raining cats and dogs" basically means that it's raining outside. That is a phrase as well as an idiom. By learning such phrases, you're able to converse more naturally and you're able to understand the meaning.

In addition, the endings of words often change according to the sentence. By learning a range of different common phrases, you'll be able to converse far more easily, but you'll also make sure that you're speaking correct English, and not broken English. Someone who speaks broken English is not fluent, they are simply getting by. That isn't your aim.

"How are you?" Is a phrase, and probably one of the most common you will hear and use. If you break the words down individually, they don't seem to make sense together. Asking someone "how" generally means how they do something, not how they are feeling.

Commit to listening to and understanding phrases as much as words and watch your vocabulary grow as a result. Again, you can use the journal method, combining this with words, and attempting to use what you learn in general conversation.

How to Memorize Your Vocabulary

With such a huge number of words and phrases coming your way, how are you supposed to not only understand them but remember them too?

I mentioned the art of repetition earlier, and that is really your go-to option when it comes to memorizing the word and phrases you're learning. Also, you could try visualization techniques too.

For words that you're struggling to commit to memory, try and attach an image to them. For instance, if you're trying to remember the word "scalding", i.e. meaning "hot", then say the word aloud whilst visualizing a fire in your mind. Repeat it a few times and keep the image in your mind. Eventually, your memory will connect the image with the word. Whenever you see a fire, it's quite likely that the word "scalding" will pop into your mind, but when you want to remember the word you're trying to learn, simply pulling the image into your mind should trigger the word to pop up from your memory.

This is a technique that may take time, especially when you have a large number of words and phrases to remember, but it's ideal for the more difficult options and the ones which you seem to have trouble remembering in general.

Another technique is the simplest of them all. Use the words as much as possible. The more you use a word, the easier it will be to remember.

To sum up, these are the best ways to memorize your vocabulary, whilst you're attempting to build it up at the same time.

- Use new words and phrases as much as possible
- Repeat the new vocabulary additions you learn, by writing them down and looking at them daily, saying them aloud
- Use the image association method, i.e. assigning a visualized image to a word or phrase
- Use flashcards to help you pull new words from your memory, and test yourself on a regular basis

Language doesn't only hinge on grammar, it hinges on vocabulary too. Whilst you don't necessarily need to spend a large amount of time studying the nuances of the language in terms of its grammatical rules, you do need to know how to form sentences in the right way. Listening and reading is the single best way to attain fluency, and from there you can work to build up your vocabulary, giving you a greater choice of words and phrases to use in general conversation.

CHAPTER 7:

Accent Reduction Techniques

I have touched upon accents a few times throughout the book so far, but this chapter is going to focus on how to reduce your own accent, to ensure that the English you speak is crystal clear.

The fact that you come from a non-English speaking country, i.e. you have another language as your mother tongue, means that you are going to have an accent of some kind. The thickness of that accent, i.e. its strength, not only depends on where you're from, but also your regional dialect, and your voice in general. Everyone has a specific accent, whether strong or slight, and it can affect your English-speaking skills if you're not careful.

To speak English correctly, you need to pay very close attention to the way sounds are made and ensure that you copy that sound completely. The type of English accent you will adopt when speaking English really depends upon the type of material you're using when learning. For instance, if you're using shadowing and you're listening to an American English speaker, then you're going to find yourself speaking with a slight American accent yourself. Similarly, if you're listening to an Australian speak English, you'll have a slight Australian twang to your own speech. If you're listening to an English speaker from the UK, specifically England itself, your English speech will be clearer and have that traditional British sound.

Does it matter which you go for? Not necessarily. It really depends upon you and what you're trying to achieve. The words used are the same, and if you're going to be spending a lot of time in America, perhaps it is better if you shadow using exercise from an American native speaker. The choices are yours.

What you do need to focus on however is reducing your own accent to ensure that it doesn't interfere with the way you pronounce sounds and words.

Many people go to accent reduction classes, but I don't believe that is necessary. These classes can be quite expensive and don't really teach you anything other than what shadowing will already teach you. Instead, I recommend you focus on the sound of your voice and be mindful of the sounds you're making. It may take time and effort, but it will ensure that your English-speaking accent is as clear as possible and isn't affected by your native language.

Shadowing - The Number One Way to Reduce Your Accent

Firstly, it's entirely possible to reduce your own accent, but it means being very mindful of the way your mouth forms sound. The letter 'a' in the English language sounds very different between UK accents and American accents, so this is something to be mindful of.

The single best way to reduce your accent and ensure that the English you're speaking is done via an English native's accent is to use shadowing.

I talked you through the shadowing method in an earlier chapter, but let's recap now for completeness' sake.

Shadowing is:

- Listening to a passage of text via audio recording

- Understanding the meaning of the text and looking up any words you're not sure of

- Repeating the text at the same tempo (a split second behind) the native speaker and pronouncing the words in the same way

- Repeating the passage of text until it is committed to memory

Shadowing will allow you to pronounce words and phrases in the same way as the person you're listening to, and if you stick to the same person, effectively, you will copy their accent if you listen to it enough. By doing this, you're flattening out your own accent and getting rid of any inflections which may cause your English to sound a little broken or misunderstood.

The reason I recommend shadowing for accent reduction is that it is the easiest way to achieve your aim. You're not consciously attempting to change your accent in this case, you're simply listening to the way someone else pronounces words and you're copying it, gaining information from them.

Listen to Your Own Voice And be Mindful of Sounds

Another way to ensure that your accent doesn't interfere with your fluency journey is to be very mindful of the sounds you're making especially as you start to get into longer conversations. In this situation, your accent may begin to creep in because you're focusing so much on the words you're using and the back and forth element of the conversation. In this case, you may be less careful about sounds and focus more on words.

Remember, fluency isn't only about knowledge of words, but also the way you say them. You can completely ruin a conversation by not understanding pronunciation and simply attempting to say words that don't have any real similarity to how they're supposed to sound.

Tape yourself and listen to the recording back. Any time you hear your accent creeping in, re-record what you hear and attempt to right the issue. Only by being mindful and careful of the way you pronounce words can you banish your accent when speaking fluent English.

CHAPTER 8:

The Key to Mastery

By this point, you should be feeling more confident in your English-speaking skills and you should be starting to put into practice some of the exercises and techniques I've introduced you to. There is one thing which will give you the best foundation on which to build, however, and that is understanding that mastery lies in being able to repeat and repeat until you memorize and learn.

Repetition is the way we learn. I've already touched upon this, but to understand how to be fluent, you need to understand how the brain learns and commits things to memory.

Understanding The Art of Repetition

As a child, you will have learned the alphabet in your native language and you probably had to repeat it repeatedly, be it in song or chants. The reason for this isn't because your teacher didn't have anything better to teach you, it was because by repeating something continuously, your brain stores the information in your long-term memory bank. This also explains why you can hear a song on the radio a few times, and then have it stuck in your brain for days afterward.

When you hear something just once or twice, your brain acknowledges it and then forgets it quite soon afterward. There is no importance placed on this information because your brain only hears it once. You may remember it again at some point perhaps when you hear it once more, but the likelihood is that you'll simply forget. Now, if you repeat that same thing several times, and continue to repeat it daily, your brain will take this information and process it accordingly. Because it's hard this information several times, it assumes it to be important, and as a result, stores it in your long-term memory bank, where it can be pulled out of your memory regularly for use.

When learning how to speak English fluently, the main aspect of repetition comes down to pronunciation and vocabulary. I've already talked about ways to memorize vocabulary and now you understand more about how the brain learns and remembers, you'll be able to see why repetition is so important. The same goes for learning how to pronounce sounds and words. The sound of the word, when repeated, sticks in your mind and allows you to pull that information forward whenever needed.

To use this very powerful learning tool however, you need to commit time and effort to repetition, using games, songs, journals, shadowing and listening techniques, etc.

The Three Steps to Mastering English Fluency

Aside from repetition, there are three steps that you need to follow, which if done regularly, will solidify your fluency and allow you to build confidence when conversing with native English speakers.

These three steps are:

1. Speak English as often as you can, even if it means speaking to yourself in the mirror

2. Find regular opportunities to converse and practice in English

3. Have patience and don't give up

Let's look at these in turn.

Speaking English as much as possible basically pulls the repetition element into play. You're also building your confidence and allowing yourself to feel more in control when using a language that isn't your first. If you need to have imaginary conversations with yourself in the mirror, that's fine; the way you do it doesn't matter, it's simply a case of using English speech whenever you get the chance and inventing opportunities if you cannot immerse yourself in English too easily in your own setting.

Secondly, you need to find regular opportunities to converse in English if at all possible. This could be with a native English speaker you know at work or in the local supermarket, it could be speaking to a friend on social media call who lives many miles away, but you need to try your best to have as much real-time practice as possible. This will give you more confidence and will allow you to make the mistakes you need to make, so you can learn how to do better in the future.

Finally, and perhaps the most important point to make is that you need to have patience. If learning a language was easy, I wouldn't need to write a book on it. You will not have a smooth ride, and you're going to struggle at times. Having said that, having excitement and interest in English will allow you to overcome any problems you encounter.

You should also remember that mistakes aren't bad things, they're opportunities to learn. If you make a mistake when pronouncing a word, don't worry about it and certainly don't give up. Instead, focus on getting it right the next time and celebrate overcoming a hurdle. The more opportunities you have to learn from your mistakes, the better your fluency skills will be.

Why You Shouldn't Expect Miracles Overnight

Finally, do not expect miracles overnight. You can learn to speak fluent English very quickly, but you're still going to make mistakes occasionally and you will still need to look occasional words up. Come to terms with the fact that you will probably always need to use a thesaurus or look words up because you're fluent, not native! This is fine and it means you can continue learning and continue doing better.

Play the long game and you will find that results come your way, but understand that patience is the key to mastering English fluency.

BONUS: CHAPTER 9:

The Secret Method to Become Super Fluent in 21 Days

We are almost at the end of the book and that means you have all the information you need to become fluent in English. Despite that, you might feel you need a little structure, and in that case, I'm going to teach you a 21-day program, which will allow you to become fluent in English in just 21 days.

The idea is that after the 21 days (just three weeks of your time) you will be able to speak English much more confidently and certainly more fluently than before. You will also find that your accent doesn't interfere with your English speaking, because you're going to be using shadowing exercises intensively throughout the program duration.

Before I explain the program in detail, it's important to realize that this is an intensive program, and you need to dedicate time and effort to finish the tasks for every day. If you can do that, you will see results. If however you skip days and don't put the time into the program, your end results aren't going to be anywhere near what they could be. It's not easy, but the exercises themselves are simple.

Three Things You Need to Master First

The 21-day fast track method isn't for everyone, and in order to be eligible to gain results, you need to meet the following three criteria:

1. You can understand 75% of the English spoken on TV, on movies, or when you're watching YouTube videos

2. You have the opportunity to avoid speaking your mother tongue language for the full 21 days or speak as little as possible. This means you need to immerse yourself in English as much as possible

3. You can program your brain to think and speak in English for the full 21 days

If you can tick those three boxes at this time, you will find that at the end of 21 days your English fluency will be much improved to what it is now, and with more practice beyond, you will be able to reach complete fluency level in the near future.

The Guidelines of The Fast Track Method

Every single day you need to commit to a certain amount of exercise, and you need to follow the set time scales in order to get the full benefit. In addition, you also need to follow the three rules I've just mentioned above. That means avoiding speaking your native language, or use it as little as is possible, think and speak in English, therefore totally immersing yourself, and continue to try and understand at least 80% of what you see on TV or on videos you watch in English.

This intensive 21 days method will only work if you commit to following the three rules and doing the exercises set every day. It may also help to do some preparation beforehand, i.e. gathering enough material to shadow and listen or read. By doing that, you will find that you have less time spent looking for things, and more time to practice and focus.

It might be a good idea to explain to those around you what you're going to do, to help you avoid having to discuss things in your mother tongue language. The idea behind the fast track method is that it is completely immersive, and if you're dipping in and out of different languages you may find yourself a little confused, therefore affecting your results. In addition, if you're currently working in your home country, book some vacation time and allow yourself the space to be able to focus on your language effects as much as possible.

The program focuses on listening to passages of text via video or audio recording, so if you want to make life a little easier, gather several podcasts or YouTube videos of around 10 to 20 minutes in length and have them to one side for when you begin your exercises.

It may seem like a large sacrifice, but it is one that is more than worth making if you want to achieve your dream of English fluency.

The Fast Track Method Explained - 21 Days to Fluency

Throughout the 21 days of the fast track method, you need to do the following exercises every single day:

Intensive listening - 2 hours

Every day for 2 hours you need to do intensive listening exercises. This means listening to a short YouTube video or a short podcast and focusing on what is being said.

If you need a reminder on what intensive listening is, you can recap on my earlier chapter, but overall this is spending short bursts of time listening to short videos or recordings and listening to how words are pronounced, and how sentences are structured. It's a good idea to choose a video or recording which you're interested in, i.e. a subject which you like, as this will make it easier to understand and completely immerse yourself in what is being said.

Choose videos or podcasts which are around 10 to 20 minutes long, but no longer than that. Don't just listen to the words, listen to how they are said, and how every single word and phrase links together. To successfully tick the day's exercise off your list, you need to work somewhere quiet, where you're not going to be disturbed. In order to listen correctly, your mind needs to be on what you're listening to completely.

You should do this for 2 hours in one straight block and listen to the content on repeat for that time. By the end of the session, you will be able to say the content yourself, but you will also have learned a lot about phrases, vocabulary, and pronunciation.

Shadowing - 2 hours

Every day you also need to commit to shadowing. Again, I covered exactly what shadowing is in an earlier chapter, but this is the part of the program which will ensure your accent is reduced, that you can pronounce words correctly, and will also allow you to understand idioms and slang a little too.

Choose a video or podcast which interests you, to make sure that you stay on target and understand the content correctly. Listen to it through a couple of times before you begin speaking, to ensure that you understand what is being said. If there are any words you're not sure of, look them up at this point. When you're ready, begin speaking. This means repeating the words back at the same tempo as the speaker, paying special attention to the pronunciation of letters and words.

By the end of the 2-hour block, you will know this passage off by heart and if you don't, you haven't done it correctly!

And that's it. Just four hours every day and two techniques that will teach you English fluency. Of course, you need to follow the three rules mentioned above also, otherwise, the program will not be as effective for you.

Think in English, speak in English, and you will probably find that halfway through the program you begin to dream in English too. This program is ideal for anyone who struggles to immerse themselves in English in their regular day to day routine. If you live in a country that doesn't have many native English speakers and you're attempting to become fluent, it's very difficult to learn if you can't cut yourself off from your mother tongue and think and speak in your new language. This program will allow you to do that, but it will only work if you follow the three guidelines above.

What can you expect at the end of the 21 days? An increased level of fluency for sure. You will have learned new words, have an increased vocabulary, your accent will have reduced, and you will have a lot more confidence when speaking the language to native speakers.

The fact that you have spoken and thought in English for 21 days may make you feel a little strange when you go back to speaking your native language, but that is just proof of how well you did during the three weeks immersive work.

Will you be completely, 100% fluent? Possibly not, but you will have made huge strides forward, and you will be as close as it is possible to get. With extra work in the future, albeit on a less intensive basis as the last three weeks, you will have the ultimate confidence when speaking English at a fluent level.

Conclusion

We have now reached the end of our fluency journey together and I hope that at this point you're feeling energized and hopeful of achieving your own fluency level. If you have followed the 21-day program and you're now reading the conclusion to the book, you should be able to testify just how successful the techniques I have explained are for anyone who wants to become fluent in the English language.

If you're yet to embark upon the 21-day program, focus and be patient, giving your all to the four hours of practice that you need to do every single day, whilst also immersing yourself in the English speech and thought process. It may seem like a lot to take in, but becoming fluent in any language means reaching a high level of excellence. In order to do that, you need to focus and ensure that you put in the effort to grab the results in your favor.

Thank you for reading Advanced English Fluency Explained. I hope you found the content helpful and I hope that it gave you the confidence to go forth and conquer your new language skills.

Being fluent in any language is difficult but it is also something which is attainable by everyone, provided they put forth the time and effort. Being fluent in English will help you to hold deeper and more meaningful conversations with those around you, and it will allow you to indulge in the small talk too, which is a vital part of everyday life.

Whether you're planning on moving to a native English speaking country, or you want to learn fluent English perhaps for work, the techniques I have explained in this book are the best to get you to your final destination. Whilst achieving native speaking level is extremely difficult, fluency is within your reach.

The most important thing you need to remember is A for attitude. When learning any language, attitude is everything. Having a positive and hard-working attitude when it comes to learning language means that you won't give up when things get a little difficult. There are going to be things you don't understand, which need a little extra repetition in order to gain that understanding. There are going to be words which you find hard to pronounce, but practice really does make perfect.

It's vital that you do not give up when these hurdles come your way, and that you put forth the effort requires. Nothing comes easy, and when learning a language that is a truth. If you work hard and follow the 21-day program rules however, fluency will come to you.

Finally, it's important to remember that once you achieve fluency level, you should continue speaking as much as possible. A second language doesn't stay in your mind forever, and if you don't use it, you will lose it. Remember, we learn by repetition, but we need to continue repeating by use if we want to keep those words and phrases in our minds. Speak in English whenever you can, practice by listening and using shadowing on a regular basis, even after you've finished the 21-day program, and understand that there is always more to learn.

English is a language that is full of contradictions. Rules don't always ring true, there are always new idioms popping up, which make no sense and bear no real meaning to the words spoken, and new slang is emerging every second. Your language journey will probably never end, but isn't that the most exciting thing? There is always more to do, always more to learn!

At this point, I will bid you goodbye and wish you luck in your English fluency journey. Work hard, don't give up, have patience, and practice as much as you can. If you can do that, English fluency most certainly will be yours.

Dear English Learners:

Thank you for reading "The Black Book of Speaking Fluent English". I hope you enjoyed and find this book helpful, please take some time to share this book with your friends and families. It would also be nice if you are able to leave a positive review, even if it's <u>only a line or two</u>; it would make all the difference and would be greatly appreciated.

Thank you,

Your Advanced English Teacher -- Christopher Hill

www.ingramcontent.com/pod-product-compliance
Lightning Source LLC
Chambersburg PA
CBHW060406080526
44583CB00012B/490